Wisdom To Succeed Workbook

Welcome!

Welcome to your wisdom workbook. Here you will receive advice and action steps to incorporate into your life and business. You will walk away empowered to make wise decisions, manage your time, succeed in business, hit your goals, live your dreams, and live your life to the fullest.

Do you want to be wise?

I'm guessing your answer is yes because you bought this workbook. But in order to reap the full benefits of this workbook, you need to be ALL IN! This workbook is a dig-deep, lay-it-all-out-on-the-table, ask-the-tough-questions, and put-the-puzzle-pieces-together to create your masterpiece for success.

Let's start by positioning ourselves correctly with open hearts and minds. Then ask God for wisdom and solutions to our problems. And He will give us wisdom!

Psalm 84:10 RSV states, "For a day in thy courts is better than a thousand elsewhere..." Spending time with God in this course is more beneficial than spending a thousand days elsewhere! Fifteen minutes with God every day in this workbook is better than 250 hours spent elsewhere in using your own power. This workbook based on God's Word gives you a great return on your investment (ROI).

Be Expectant

When you ask for wisdom, make sure your faith is in God alone because you cannot expect to receive anything if you are divided between God and the world.

Hebrews 11:5-6 in The Message Translation says that it's impossible to please God apart from faith because anyone who wants to approach Him must believe that He exists and that He cares enough to respond to those who seek Him.

We must have faith that He exists and will respond to us, and then we need to ask Him.

Ask Him to give you an open heart and mind to receive wisdom and heavenly solutions. Take some time here and ask God for wisdom in specific areas where you need help.

p: Foundation of Wisdom

Remove Limiting Thoughts and Beliefs

At this point you might be saying, well I have failed in the past, how is this time going to be different? You might even be saying, "This is too much," or "I can't do this." Stop right there and throw out the negative, limiting thoughts and beliefs. Instead, focus on the positive. You can do this! God is for you. And every past failure is a teaching and training ground where you learned valuable lessons to take you to the next level.

The book of James tells us that God covers our failures with His generous grace. Take time to thank God for His generous grace and wisdom that He is giving you right now. If there have been past failures, declare that God is covering those failures with His grace and turning them around for your good. This is your year for success.

Lay the Foundation

In buildings and homes, the foundation must be solid and built correctly to hold the weight and height of the building. If the foundation is faulty and a storm comes, the building will crumble.

The fear of the Lord is the foundation of wisdom for this course. And fear is the reverence of the Lord and the actions and character that come from respect and love for Him. Wisdom, knowledge, and understanding flow from this place.

Proverbs 1:7 NLT says, "The fear of the Lord is the foundation of true knowledge, but fools despise wisdom and discipline."

Get ready to dive into Proverbs these next few weeks and receive wisdom, create a disciplined life, take action, and receive understanding of the insights of the wise. Your hard work will reap incredible rewards of life, prosperity, favor, and success.

IT'S GO TIME!

p:Gaining Knowledge

Knowledge

The beginning of true knowledge is fear of the Lord and obedience to Him. He is our foundation.

Knowing is awareness of facts and skills. Knowing is being familiar with something through experience or study.

Needing knowledge applies to other areas of our lives as well. For example, if you want to start a business, you need knowledge of the industry, your target market, your competitive advantage, and your competitors. You will do research and study to gain knowledge. You might even intern with a company to receive knowledge through experience.

Today, we are going to research God's word to gain knowledge.

Proverbs 1:5 TPT says, "For the wise, these proverbs will make you even wiser, and for those with discernment, you will be able to acquire brilliant strategies for leadership."

Get excited for the Lord to give you brilliant strategies to lead and to become even wiser! Ask the Lord right now for a a brilliant strategy to lead! Reflect on leadership qualities such as integrity, character, and honesty.

As a leader, pay attention to those around you. Who you associate with makes a difference in your success. We all know the saying that you are known by the company you keep.

One piece of advice from Proverbs 1:10 is to turn your back on sinners if they try to entice you. The Message translation says it this way, "If bad companions tempt you, don't go along with them."

Bad companions are those who try and grab whatever they can get at other people's expense. They are selfish, greedy, and hungry to ruin everything they lay their hands on. They are careless, and carelessness kills!

p: Gaining Knowledge

As wise individuals, we cannot be careless, or complacent. Choose wise advisors for your business. Choose wise mentors for your life. Choose wise friends for your life. Who surrounds you? What's their character? What's your character?

Do not be smug

Proverbs warns us not to be smug. We need open hearts and open ears to hear God and to receive His advice, counsel, wisdom, and knowledge. So don't be a know-it-all!

Proverbs 1:32 TPT says, "Like an idiot you've turned away from me and chosen destruction instead. Your self-satisfied smugness will kill you."

Don't be an idiot and turn away from the Lord. Don't be greedy or try living on your own without God. I tried living without God and that led to destruction. But He is quick to forgive, redeem, and restore. He did it for me and will do the same for you.

There is more amazing news! Proverbs 1:33 TPT says, "But the one who always listens to me will live undisturbed in a heavenly peace. Free from fear, confident and courageous, that one will rest unafraid and sheltered from the storms of life."

What an incredible promise and gift. Take some time to meditate on this promise for yourself. Thank the Lord that by always listening to Him, you live undisturbed in a heavenly peace. You are fearless. You are confident. You are courageous. You rest unafraid. And you are sheltered from the storms of life.

Declare it:

p: Gaining Knowledge

Notes:

p: Applying Wisdom

Applying Wisdom

Proverbs 2 commences with how to apply wisdom:

First, we need to listen to what God says. Second, we speak. And third, we act.

This same instruction applies to other relationships and to business as well. We listen, then we speak and act. We gain knowledge on a topic through researching, listening to podcasts, and reading books. Then we can speak and act on that knowledge.

For example, if you want to purchase a home, you may hire a realtor and listen to their advice. You may visit the neighborhood, search for homes, or listen to a podcast on purchasing your first home. You then apply the knowledge you receive to make a wise purchase.

James 1:19-21 tells us that once we hear, then we act on what we hear.

So first, we listen to the Lord. Psalm 25:14 TPT says, "There's a private place reserved for the lovers of God where they sit near Him and receive the revelation secrets of His promises."

Take some time today and sit with the Lord. Ask Him a question and listen. Then take action. Here are a couple examples:

Lord, what is the task you are setting before me today?

_____

_____

Lord, what is a promise you have for me?

_____

_____

If you are feeling stuck on these questions, or don't think you hear God's voice, read on for some tips on how to hear God's voice. You do hear Him! And you can train your heart to listen to Him.

p: Applying Wisdom

Notes:

Train Your Heart To Listen

Proverbs 2:2 tells us to train our hearts to listen when God speaks and to open our spirits wide to expand our discernment. Then we are to pass on what we hear to our sons and daughters.

Proverbs 2:2-3 TPT "So train your heart to listen when I speak and open your spirit wide to expand your discernment—then pass it on to your sons and daughters. Yes, cry out for comprehension and intercede for insight."

NLT says "Tune your ears to wisdom and concentrate on understanding. Cry out for insight and ask for understanding."

As we continue in Proverbs 2, God tells us to search for knowledge, understanding, and wisdom as we would for hidden treasures. The Lord grants wisdom, knowledge, and understanding to the honest. He holds success in store for the upright.

Ask the tough questions: Are you honest? Upright? God holds success for you. He created you for greatness. Ask the Lord for wisdom.

With wisdom, you will know and understand what is right, just, and fair. You will know every good path. And wisdom will save you from the ways of wicked people and from seductive words.

Let's take a minute and train our hearts and ears to listen to the Lord. Start by sitting in a quiet place with no distractions. You will start hearing God as you are working, driving, cleaning, resting, and walking.

The first couple of times you do this exercise, say out loud "In the name of Jesus, I silence all other voices. I hear your voice Lord and it is peaceful and packed with wisdom for my hope and betterment. I open my heart to you Lord. I receive your wisdom, instruction, and knowledge."

Say your name in your mind, not out loud. This is what God's voice will sound like to you. He will give you His thoughts, and His thoughts are so much higher than our thoughts.

p:Train Your Heart To Listen

In summary:

- We listen for God's voice.
- We ask the Lord a question and listen to the answer before responding or completing the task God gave us.
- We are attentive and hang on to God's every word.
- We incline our hearts to His voice, knowledge, and insight and then apply what we hear with faith.
- Application is obedience, and the result is good fruit.

A hypocrite hears and knows, yet follows the world and does not apply/do what he hears and knows. So let's be doers of the Word.

James 1:22 NIV says, "Do not merely listen to the word, and so deceive yourselves. Do what it says."

Matthew 7:24 says, "Therefore anyone who hears these words of mine and acts on them is like a wise man who built his house on the Rock."

Let's apply the words we received today to our daily lives. Today what is one thing the Lord gave you to complete? Write down what the Lord gave you and complete it.

9 Rewards of Wisdom
Read Proverbs 3:1-18

Proverbs 3 is packed full of rewards of wisdom. Here, I will highlight 9 rewards:

1. Long and Satisfying Life

Never forget what God teaches you. Store His commands and teachings in your heart. If you do this, you will live longer, and your life will be more satisfying.

2. Find Favor with God and Man

Never let loyalty and kindness leave you; write them deep within your heart. The Amplified translation says to let loyalty and kindness define you. Then you will find favor with God and man, and you will earn a good reputation!

3. Direction

God will show you which way to go in life and in business. "Trust in the Lord with all your heart; do not depend on your own understanding. Seek his will in all you do, and he will show you which path to take." Proverbs 3:5-6 NLT

4. Health

Proverbs 3:7-8 AMP says, "Do not be wise in your own eyes. Fear the Lord with reverent awe and obedience and turn entirely away from evil. It will be health to your body, your marrow, your nerves, your sinews, your muscles, all your inner parts and refreshment (physical well-being) to your bones."

The same verse in NLT says, "Don't be impressed with your own wisdom. Instead, fear the Lord and turn away from evil. Then you have healing for your body and strength for your bones.

5. Wealth

Proverbs 3:9-10 NLT says, "Honor the Lord with your wealth and with the best part of everything you produce." The AMP translation says, "honor the Lord with your wealth and income." NKJV says, "honor the Lord with your possessions."

Then you will overflow with new wine (joy) and your barns (shelter, food, animals, business) will be filled.

Giving and honoring the Lord with our wealth gives us joy and abundance!

"Then your barns will be abundantly filled and your vats will overflow with new wine." Proverbs 3:10 AMP

"Then every dimension of your life will overflow with blessings from an uncontainable source of inner joy!" Proverbs 3:10 TPT

6. Correction and Instruction

The Lord's correction and instruction are better than any father on earth can give his child.

God tells us to not refuse the Lord's correction and instruction. Who the Lord loves, He corrects! He leads us on straight and pleasant paths. He leads us to abundant life. If God is correcting you, it's to save you and make you better.

7. Happiness and Blessings

Wisdom gives understanding! The gain from wisdom is far better than getting gold Proverbs 16:16.

Wisdom is a tree of life to those who take hold of her! And happy is everyone who retains her.

8. Long Life and Honor

Wisdom gives us long life in one hand and wealth and promotion in the other hand. Proverbs 3:16 KJV says "Length of days is in her right hand; and in her left hand riches and honor."

9. Sweet and Pleasant Ways

Wisdom gives us sweet and pleasant ways. All her paths are peace. Wisdom gives wholeness, peace, and prosperity.

Wow! There are so many rewards from finding and taking hold of wisdom. Take some time today and meditate on the rewards that stand out to you.

Thank the Lord for His wisdom. And ask the Lord for His wisdom throughout each day.

----

p:Rewards of Wisdom

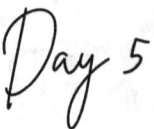

Notes:

"Wisdom and wealth go hand-in-hand. Wealth without wisdom is foolishness."
                                    - Juanita Weldon, Owner of Sonoran Desert Oasis

p: How To Get Wisdom

How to Get Wisdom

Proverbs 4 tells us to 'get wisdom.' So how do we get wisdom?

Proverbs 4:5 NLT "Get wisdom; develop good judgment. Don't forget my words or turn away from them."

When I read Proverbs 4, God reminded me of the parable Jesus told about the wise man who built his house on the rock and the foolish man who built his house on the sand. When the wind, rain, and pressure came, the house on the sand washed away, but the house on the solid rock stood firm!

1. Build a Solid Foundation

The foundation of wisdom is the fear (reverence) of the Lord and having Him as your solid foundation. When your roots are deep in Him, you can withstand the storms of life.

This parable applies to our faith, work, and sports. We need a solid foundation in our faith, which is Christ and His finished work on the cross. When pressures in life come, our faith holds firm if it is in Christ and His finished work.

If we have built our faith on something else and pressures and trials come, we will sink and get tossed back and forth by the winds of life.

In order to withstand pressure, adversity, and trials in business, we need a solid foundation. Also, we need to know the fundamentals of the business. If we master the fundamentals of the business and have a proven business model, we will be able to stand in the storm.

In sports, we need the fundamentals ingrained in us, so that when the pressure of the defense comes, we can leap over it or pass through it.

p: How To Get Wisdom

2. Search, Seek, and Ask

Another way to get wisdom is to seek, search, and ask for wisdom.

Seek first the Kingdom of God and His righteousness and all these things will be added to you Matthew 6:33. We seek God first, which means we ask Him first for guidance and wisdom. We search His word in order to gain a competitive advantage in business. We search and research to become an expert in our field and know our competition.

3. Have Mentors

A third way to get wisdom is to find mentors. The Holy Spirit is our best mentor. He is our advocate and teacher. The Holy Spirit also uses other people to confirm what He is saying. Also, remember that in Jesus are hid all the treasures of wisdom and knowledge Colossians 2:3. So it's important to spend daily time with Jesus.

4. Gain Experience

Experience is another way to gain wisdom. We cannot just be hearers of the word, but we need to be doers of the word. Obeying God demonstrates wisdom. Stepping out and doing what God asks you to do is a sign of maturity. As you step out and do things, such as start a business or compete in sports, you learn from your experiences. You take what is good and discard what is bad.

What is an action you took that led to success?

_____

Thank the Lord for His wisdom and guidance. Pick one specific way to get wisdom and incorporate it into your daily life. After that has become a habit, pick another one to incorporate into your daily life.

_____

_____

_____

_____

Wise Advice for Life and Business

Read Proverbs 4:24-27 in three different translations.

These four verses give us insight and wise advice on how to honor God and live life to the fullest.

1. Avoid all perverse talk. Stay away from corrupt, false, and crooked speech. Don't talk negatively about yourself or others.

2. Be honest in all things. You will grow in favor and stature with God and man.

3. Look straight ahead with a FIXED PURPOSE. Know your purpose and stand firm in it! What's your purpose? And what is your plan to stand firm in it?

Part of your purpose is for God to raise you up to show His power in and through you. Remember, God created you for greatness. Exodus 9:16 Amp says, "But indeed for this very reason I have allowed you to live, in order to show you My power and in order that My name may be proclaimed throughout all the earth."

Believe in your purpose against all odds and be ready for your purpose to be tested. Others around you might say you can't do it, so you need to silence the negative voices and stand firm in your purpose. This testing produces endurance, character, perseverance, and hope.

Be intentional with what you speak from your mouth, and be intentional with your decisions. Are they leading you toward your purpose? Are they building you up or tearing you down?

---

p: Wise Advice for Life and Business *Day 7*

Looking straight ahead includes having a vision, mission, goals, and a business plan and/or life plan to achieve your purposes on earth.

Write out a business plan. Research one-page business plans for ideas and consider the questions below. Commit your business plan to the Lord for He will mark out a straight path for you to take.

Proverbs tell us to ponder our path and weigh it mentally. Ask God for wisdom and direction. Wisdom helps us stay on the safe path. The safe path has God as the leader.

Where are you going?

_____

_____

Where do you want to go?

_____

_____

How will you get there?

_____

_____

What are your short-term goals?

_____

_____

What are your long-term goals?

_____

_____

What is your plan to achieve those goals?

_____

Will your contemplated action move you closer to your goals or further from them?

_____

4. Don't get sidetracked. Stay focused. Keep your feet from following evil.
This is where your short-term goals will help you! Time management will accelerate your growth.

Make a daily goal and a plan to achieve it. This will help you stay on track and accomplish your purposes in life. Here is an example of one of my daily plans:

Today I Want to Accomplish:	Today I Want to Accomplish:
• time with the Lord 30 min-hour (every day starts this way) • listen to one podcast on real estate or business • 1 hour activity with my kids • analyze 2 properties • search 10-15 properties • walk with my husband • 30 min workout • one write up for podcast	• • • • • • • • •
Jane's Daily Plan	My Daily Plan

Include your core values in your business plan and/or life plan. For example, you might list honesty or integrity. You want to make sure that these values are part of who you are and how you do business and live life, not just a list on a piece of paper. If you list honesty as a core value and later a lucrative, yet dishonest business deal comes your way, say no! This type of deal will lead to destruction, and dishonesty is not part of who you are or what you value.

Stand firm in who you are in Christ and your purpose.

Take some time today to think through these questions and strategies, so that you may be fruitful in all things and stay on track to accomplish your purpose.

Notes:

p: Avoid Immorality

Avoid Immorality

Read Proverbs 5:1-7.

Pay attention and listen to God's wisdom because it leads to abundant life. Listening to immorality leads to death in your relationships, business dealings, and what you want to accomplish in life.

To listen to God's wisdom in the Strong's Concordance means: to be wise in mind, words, and actions and to be skillful, witty, and wise.

Jesus was skillful, witty, and always had a perfect answer. I think we can all say that we would like to be skillful, wise, and witty in life and business. So here is some advice from Proverbs 5 to apply to your life and business to achieve success:

We need to be wise in our minds, in what we speak, and in what we do!

First, think (listen), then speak, and then act. First, yield your ear to God's understanding, intelligence, reason, discretion, and skillfulness. Then you can show discernment and your lips will express what you learned. You will speak skillfully with wise advice and with intelligence. You will speak as an upright leader in your family, business, area of influence, and city!

p: Importance of Listening

Why is listening to God's wisdom and having discernment so important?

1. People "smooth talk" you.

The lips of an immoral woman are sweet as honey. In Strong's Concordance, an immoral woman means more than a woman trying to sexually seduce you. Yes, stay pure and avoid immoral women, but an immoral woman in Hebrew also refers to a stranger, another person, and heresy. Do not take advice from immoral strangers or immoral people, because their advice leads to a bitter end.

Immoral advice and immorality are poison and will slowly kill you and your relationships. Proverbs says immorality and immoral advice lead to a bitter future. God warns us that immoral advice may seem good at the moment (smooth talk), but it is as sharp as a two-edged sword. This means bitterness can penetrate deep into you and slowly kill you.

Don't self-destruct. Get rid of all bitterness, envy, and rage. Repent of it and fill yourself with God's word, which "is living and active, sharper than any two-edged sword, piercing to the division of soul and of spirit, of joints and of marrow, and discerning the thoughts and intentions of the heart (Hebrews 4:12 ESV)."

There are two options in this Proverb. One, you can follow immoral advice, which will lead you on the path to death and straight to the grave because "she" cares nothing about the path of life. "She" staggers, and she doesn't realize it.

Two, you can choose God's word and wisdom and let them penetrate deep into every part of you. Wisdom and wise advice bring life, healing, discernment, and a smooth path.

2. Strangers take advantage.

Proverbs 5:7-14 tell us to listen to wisdom. Listen to God. Never stray from what I am about to say: Stay away from immorality. Don't go near the door of her house. Don't be seduced. Don't waste your life among the hardhearted. Don't allow strangers to take advantage of you. Why be exploited by those who care nothing for you?!

3. When you give in to immorality, you lose your honor and wealth.

If you give in to immorality, you will not only lose your honor, but also all you have achieved. Strangers will consume your wealth. Someone else will enjoy the fruits of your labor. In the end, you will groan in anguish when disease consumes your body. You will say, "How I hated discipline. If only I had not ignored all the warnings! Oh, why didn't I listen to my teachers? Why didn't I pay attention to my instructors? Why didn't I pay attention to God's Word?"

If you are currently following the immoral path, there is good news for you. God forgives, heals, restores, and redeems. He gives us a choice. You can choose Him and the path of life today and receive His healing, forgiveness, and restoration, or you can choose the immoral path that leads to destruction and death of relationships, businesses, ideas, and health.

I know this is true because I once followed the immoral path and lost my business, honor, wealth, and even became physically sick. But when I asked God for forgiveness and followed His path, He restored my destiny and purposes, healed my body, restored my honor (double portion), restored my business, and gave me a new name!

Take some time to ask the Holy Spirit if there is any bitterness or immorality in you. Ask for forgiveness and receive God's cleansing and life-giving water.

Ask the Holy Spirit if there are boundaries you need to set in your business and personal life and then implement them. Read Joel 2:25.

Thank the Lord for His wisdom, guidance, discernment, restoration, and healing!

p: Live a Disciplined Life

Lessons for Daily Living

Read Proverbs 6:1-11.

Here are three lessons to help you succeed in life and business:

1. Don't get trapped by the hunter.

If you co-sign a loan for an acquaintance and guarantee their debt, you will be sorry you did. Quickly get out of it! Get your name off the contract.

2. Consider the consequences of your decisions.

Review and consider the consequences of a business deal and/or your daily decisions before obligating yourself.

3. Don't be lazy.

"Take a lesson from the ants, you lazybones. Learn from their ways and become wise." Proverbs 6:6 NLT

Ants do not have any ruler over them to make them work, yet they labor hard all summer gathering food for the winter. They know that laziness leads to poverty.

If you are lazy, scarcity will attack you like an armed robber.

Take another lesson from the ants: no one should have to tell you what to do. LEARN SELF-DISCIPLINE.

Self-discipline
Self-discipline is a conscious control oriented toward successful outcomes by overcoming obstacles.

Example: Choosing first to complete a work assignment or school assignment before watching TV. You overcame the temptation of watching TV so you can complete your work. The only time play comes before work is in the dictionary.

p: Live a Disciplined Life

You can learn self-discipline, and God will help you! His Spirit includes self-control.

Self-discipline will keep you focused on reaching your goals, helping you manage your time and money, and keeping you healthy.

Here are some tips to help you learn self-discipline. Remember, God's Spirit gives you self-control, energy, and power,

1. Ask God to give you awareness of your choices and decisions. What choices are good? Why are they good? What past choices were bad and why?

2. Know your WHY! Knowing the why for your life and business is crucial for success because when trials come, your why will allow you to push through them.

3. Develop or review your life plan and/or business plan.

4. Set goals and list the action steps that you can implement to reach those goals.

5. Don't despise the day of small beginnings.

Think of starting a business like climbing Mount Everest. When one sets out to climb Mount Everest, one must adjust to each new level of elevation before advancing higher. If a climber climbs too fast and doesn't pause, allowing for time to adjust, their body will negatively react to the elevation changes.

Similarly, if a business climbs too fast without the proper adjustments, it can crash.

6. Establish healthy boundaries.

7. Block out time each day to think and set goals.

8. Know your identity in Christ and write out truths as declarations for the year, such as:

"I am a child of God. I am royal."
"I am smart and have the mind of Christ."
"I enjoy working to reach my goals."
"I am a successful business owner. I am an upright leader."

Isn't it amazing how much wisdom for life and business is in 11 verses?!

p: Live a Disciplined Life

Look back at past decisions and deals. Which decisions were successful and why?

Pick 2 self-discipline tips that you can implement this month.

Pick one business lesson and write down a piece of wisdom you received.

Past Decisions That Were Successful:	2 Self-Discipline Tips to Implement This Month:
• • • •	 • •

A business lesson I learned and the Wisdom I received, and as a result, I will...

_____

_____

_____

_____

_____

_____

_____

_____

_____

_____

Wisdom to Rule and Reign in Life and Business

Wisdom calls out and raises her voice to us. In the previous chapters, we learned that the harlot/voice of immorality calls out, too. You have a choice to make between listening to Wisdom's voice or that of the temptress. One leads to life and success, and one leads to destruction and death of relationships, health, business deals, and dreams.

If you want wisdom, you may be asking some of these questions: Where do I find wisdom? What is wisdom like? How do I receive wisdom? And what is the result of wisdom?

Proverbs 8 tells us that wisdom stands on the hilltop; she is not in the dark like the harlot. Wisdom was formed in the beginning before God created anything else. Wisdom was there when God established the heavens and drew the horizon on the oceans. Wisdom was the architect at God's side. Therefore, there is wisdom in creation!

Creation speaks to our hearts and minds. You can find, learn, and receive wisdom from creation. Previously, we learned from the ways of the ants and became wise. Also, you can find wisdom in listening to God's voice. He speaks to you through your thoughts (conscience), His word, and through other people. Wisdom dwells in us. Therefore, we have constant access to wisdom. We can receive and take hold of it at anytime during the day or night.

What Wisdom is:
- more valuable than rubies
- advice that is wholesome, not devious
- plain to anyone with understanding
- clear to those with knowledge (fear of the Lord is the beginning of knowledge)
- revelation to do noble things and to rule and reign in life
- good judgment
- knowledge and discernment
- common sense and success

p: Rule and Reign

Listen to Wisdom and choose wisdom over silver.
Let's examine a couple examples from history:

Solomon	Judas Iscariot
What did Solomon choose/ask for? What was the result?	What did Judas Iscariot choose/ask for? What was the result?

Solomon asked God for wisdom. In return, God gave him more than he asked for. He gave him wisdom, wealth, and honor. He told Solomon that in his lifetime he would have no equal among kings. And if he obeyed the Lord, he would give him a long life. Solomon reigned as king for 40 years. In contrast, Judas Iscariot choose silver over the Lord. His choice ended in suicide.

The result of wisdom:
Kings and queens reign because of wisdom, and rulers make just decrees. Because of Christ's finished work on the cross, we are royalty. We are kings and queens who make just decrees.

Proverbs 8:14 TPT "You will find true success when you find me, for I have insight into wise plans that are designed just for you. I hold in my hands living understanding, courage, and strength."

Ask and search for wisdom. Love wisdom. Thank the Lord for wisdom, courage, and strength. Ask for insight into God's wise plans that are designed just for you.

Notes:

Verse seventeen says one must love wisdom to gain wisdom. God knows if it is a true love or a superficial love. A superficial love will yield superficial knowledge. But those who truly desire wisdom will search and search until they find it.

What is the result of searching for and finding wisdom?
- gain great wealth and glory
- riches of righteousness
- long, satisfying life
- increase in treasuries (better benefits than a windfall of money)
- honor and riches
- favor of the Lord
- joy
- life (find wisdom, find life)
- know God more intimately

Proverbs 8:21 TPT
"Those who love me gain great wealth and a glorious inheritance and I will fill their lives with treasures."

The NLT says, "I will fill their treasuries."

How do we receive wisdom?
1. Open heart and mind to listen
2. Ask and search
3. Have reverence for the Lord, and hate all kinds of evil
3. Watch daily at Wisdom's gates. Spend time with the Lord every day. Enter into His gates with thanksgiving and His courts with praise.
4. Wait for wisdom outside her home. Wait in God's presence for His voice. He dwells in each of us.

Don't ignore wisdom. Proverbs 8 ends with a warning. "But those who miss me, injure themselves. All who hate me love death." The result of listening to immorality and the temptress is death and destruction.

Long to hear a word from the Lord every day. Ask the Lord for a word of wisdom for today. Ask the Lord for a word for your business. Write this in your daily action plan.

p: Be Wise, Not Foolish

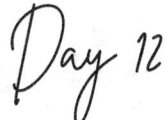

Are you Foolish or Wise?

Read Proverbs 9 and 10.

Proverbs 9 starts by telling us that Wisdom has built her house and carved its seven pillars. The seven pillars can represent the seven virtues listed in Proverbs 8 that we discussed earlier and can also refer to the seven descriptions of heavenly wisdom listed in James 3:17-18.

Wisdom that comes from heaven is:

- pure
- peace-loving
- considerate (gentle at all times)
- teachable (easy to correct, yields to others)
- full of mercy and fruit of good deeds
- impartial (no favoritism)
- sincere

If someone is sharing "wisdom" with you that does not align with the above attributes, then that wisdom is from the world and not from heaven. It's that simple. And we, as God's children, house Him!

"Do you not know and understand that you [the church] are the temple of God, and that the Spirit of God dwells [permanently] in you [collectively and individually]?

As His house, are we living the above attributes? God calls us to be pillars. Are we teachable? Sincere? Gentle at all times? Do we fear the Lord in awe, wonder, and reverence, or do we fear people and seek peoples' approval?

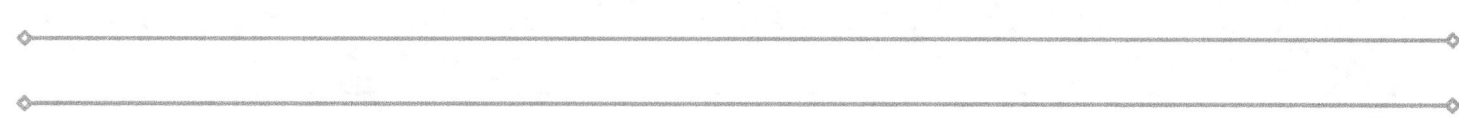

Remember, God approves you. He is for you. And His Wisdom is complete and perfect. Here is more wisdom from Proverbs 9 and 10 for life and business:

- Leave simple ways behind (receive God's wisdom and ways) and begin to live.
- Don't rebuke a mocker, you will get an insult in return.

p: Be Wise, Not Foolish

- Don't waste your time correcting the wicked, or you'll get hurt.
- Correct the wise and they will love you because they know you are saving them. Proverbs 10:17 says, "People who accept discipline are on the pathway to life, but those who ignore correction will go astray."
- Instruct the wise and they will become even wiser. Proverbs 10:8 "The wise are glad to be instructed, but babbling fools fall flat on their faces."
- Wisdom will multiply your days and add years to your life.

After describing wisdom, Proverbs 9 and 10 describe folly:

Folly will cry out as well, so be aware and on guard at all times. Folly will call out to you. Folly is foolishness and lack of good sense. Folly will lie to you and say "stolen water is refreshing" and "food eaten in secret is best." But this foolishness leads to death and destruction in relationships, health, business deals, and dreams.

The foolish will steal and cheat to gain wealth, but tainted wealth has no lasting value. Short term, the tainted wealth may seem good, but it won't last.

The foolish ignore corrections and go astray. Fools are destroyed by their lack of common sense.

Pick one or two verses from Proverbs 9 and 10 to focus on today and incorporate the point(s) into your daily life.

p: Hard Work Pays Off

Hard Work and Discipline

Proverbs 12, 13, and 14 tell us that hard work and discipline reap many rewards. In order to learn, we must first love discipline.

"To learn, you must love discipline; it is stupid to hate correction." Proverbs 12:1 NLT

You can learn to love discipline at any age. A wise child accepts a parent's discipline. Those who respect a command will succeed.

Discipline includes controlling your tongue and the words that you say. Proverbs warn us that if we open our mouths too quickly, we can ruin everything. Think before you speak. Think before you act.

The wise stay calm when insulted. How do you respond when insulted? Do you think before you respond?

⸻⸻⸻⸻⸻⸻⸻⸻⸻⸻⸻⸻⸻

⸻⸻⸻⸻⸻⸻⸻⸻⸻⸻⸻⸻⸻

Ask the Holy Spirit to help you. Be prudent, which means exercise good judgment and common sense. The prudent carefully consider their steps and avoid danger. Fools plunge ahead with reckless confidence. The prudent are crowned with knowledge and know where they are going.

Where are you going?

⸻⸻⸻⸻⸻⸻⸻⸻⸻⸻⸻⸻⸻

⸻⸻⸻⸻⸻⸻⸻⸻⸻⸻⸻⸻⸻

What are your steps to get there?

⸻⸻⸻⸻⸻⸻⸻⸻⸻⸻⸻⸻⸻

⸻⸻⸻⸻⸻⸻⸻⸻⸻⸻⸻⸻⸻

Are there any foreseeable dangers? Ask the Lord for insight.

⸻⸻⸻⸻⸻⸻⸻⸻⸻⸻⸻⸻⸻

⸻⸻⸻⸻⸻⸻⸻⸻⸻⸻⸻⸻⸻

p: Hard Work Pays Off

The Rewards of Discipline and Hard Work

Being disciplined and working hard reaps rewards. Some of the benefits of discipline and hard work include the following:

- have plenty of food
- rewards such as promotion and bounty
- prosperity
- leadership (become a leader)
- wealth grows over time
- work brings profit (mere talk leads to poverty)
- make use of everything they have without waste

Lazy people don't even cook the game they catch. They waste their talent. Don't bury your talent. It's time to rise, shine, and fulfill your dreams!

"A dream fulfilled is a tree of Life." Proverbs 13:12b NLT

What are your dreams? How can you use your talents? What is the plan to fulfill your dreams?

p: Plow Like An Ox

Put in the Work

Don't slack.

Proverbs 15:19 BSB says, "The way of the slacker is like a hedge of thorns, but the path of the upright is a highway."

"Without oxen a stable stays clean, but you need a strong ox for a large harvest."
Proverbs 14:4 NLT

"Without oxen a stall is clean, And great is the increase by the power of the ox."
Proverbs 14:4 Young's Literal Translation

Labor brings rewards, products, and revenue. Put in the work and ask God for His strength. Even in weakness, God makes you strong.

"But he said to me, "My grace is sufficient for you, for my power is made perfect in weakness." Therefore I will boast all the more gladly about my weaknesses, so that Christ's power may rest on me." 2 Corinthians 12:9 NIV

God will give you strength. He will make you plow like an ox. He makes your arms strong to bend a bow of iron. Even if you feel lost right now, or in "Egypt," God is bringing you out right now. He is giving you new strength.

"God brought them out of Egypt; They have the strength of a wild ox." Numbers 23:22 AMP

p: Plow Like An Ox

p: Joy In Your Work

Work with a Joyful Heart

"A joyful heart makes a cheerful countenance, but sorrow of the heart crushes the spirit." Proverbs 15:13 BSB

"A cheerful heart has a continual feast." Proverbs 15:15b BSB

Work from a place of love and joy. Work for the Lord, not man. Fulfill the purposes God gave you.

Proverbs 15:17 says, "Better a dish of vegetables where there is love than a fattened ox with hatred."

Remove all hatred, bitterness, and anger. Receive God's strength, joy, love, and peace. Know that God approves you and approves what you do.

"May the God of hope fill you with all joy and peace as you trust in him, so that you may overflow with hope by the power of the Holy Spirit." Romans 15:13

"Go, eat your food with gladness, and drink your wine with a joyful heart, for God has already approved what you do."

Ask the Lord for His joy. Take five minutes and sit in His presence. In God's presence is the fullness of Joy (Psalm 16:11).

p: Noble Purposes

Created For Noble Purposes
Read Romans 6:12-14.

So now we yield our bodies to God as one who has experienced resurrection life.

Remember, you have been raised from the dead and ascended to the right hand of God. You are now seated in heavenly places, reigning with Christ Ephesians 2:6.

We now live for His pleasure, not sin pleasure.

We are ready to co-labor with Him and use our bodies and skills for noble purposes. Romans 6:13 says to use your whole body as an instrument to do what is right for the glory of God. We need to use all of our members (parts of our bodies and all of our abilities) as instruments of righteousness.

Write down the abilities that you have that can be used as instruments of righteousness. How are you co-laboring with the Lord? (Remember, we operate from a place of rest in the Lord):

_____

_____

_____

Think of how the different parts of our bodies are instruments of righteousness and write them down:
Examples:
- Our feet carry the good news of the gospel
- Our feet walk us to our next business meeting
- Our hands are pure and one with the Lord, so as we lay hands on the sick, they become well
- Our hands build, write, and draw

_____

_____

Keep yourself pure for honorable use! Additional reading on this topic: Timothy 2:21-26.

p: Grab Hold Of Your Vision

Keep Your Eyes Fixed on Your Vision

"Sensible people keep their eyes glued on wisdom, but a fool's eyes wander to the ends of the earth." Proverbs 17:24 NLT

Wisdom is not a one-time deal. In life and business, we need continual wisdom. We need to keep our eyes fixed on the end goal. Keep your eyes fixed on the vision.

Have your vision and goals in front of you. Make a vision board. Add some ideas below:

```




```

Don't shrink your vision and ideas to other people's low-level thinking. Go after your purpose and destiny even when others don't believe in you. Have a victorious mindset like king David when he defeated Goliath. His brother told him to go back to tending sheep. David chose not to listen to his brother's negative voice 1 Samuel 17:42-51. Instead, he listened to God's voice. He fulfilled one of his purposes on earth and defeated Goliath! Goliath can represent obstacles, evil, or negative thinking (all of which you can conquer).

Give yourself a timeline for your goals and action steps. Have accountability to keep you on track to reach your goals. For example,

Goal: Launch an entrepreneurial business in 6 months
Action Steps: Month 1-research startups and competitors, month 2-build website
Accountability: A friend, mentor, or spouse who will check in with you once a month

Goal: Lose 10 pounds in 6 months
Action Steps: Workout 20 minutes per day/5 days per week. Eat more vegetables, and join a workout course
Accountability: a course instructor who keeps you on track, or a friend to workout with (If you forget that your goal is to lose 10 pounds in 6 months, you might start skipping your workouts. Therefore, having an accountability person is critical.)

p: Grab Hold Of Your Vision

Your turn! List a goal, action steps, and an accountability plan:

Goal:

<hr />

<hr />

Action Steps:

<hr />

<hr />

Accountability:

<hr />

<hr />

Speak positively about your goals and action steps.
Proverbs 18:21 NLT "The tongue can bring death or life; those who love to talk will reap the consequences."

Make positive declarations:

p: Diligent Not Hasty

Haste Makes Mistakes

Proverbs 19:2 NLT "Enthusiasm without knowledge is no good; haste makes mistakes."

When we hurry our steps, we can miss the mark, or go astray. We need knowledge. We need to use our knowledge. And we need wisdom on how to and when to use that knowledge.

Ask the Lord if there is an area where you need to gain knowledge. How and when does he want you to use that knowledge. Then add your enthusiasm to that knowledge.

_____

_____

_____

_____

Proverbs 19:3 NLT "People ruin their lives by their own foolishness and then are angry at the Lord."

To avoid foolishness, get wisdom. Get all the advice and instruction you can so you will be wise for the rest of your life. Plans succeed through good counsel.

Surround yourself with wise people and surround yourself with people who support you and your vision. We become wise by walking with the wise. Associate with fools and you will get into trouble. Stay away from fools because with them you won't find any knowledge.

Who do you surround yourself with? Do you have trusted mentors and friends?

_____

_____

_____

_____

Avoid hasty decisions in life and business by taking time to receive advice from the Lord, wise mentors, and friends who have knowledge and expertise in the area of business you are pursuing.

p: Diligent Not Hasty

Ask the Lord for advice on an upcoming decision:

◇————————————————————————————————◇

◇————————————————————————————————◇

Who could you connect with in your industry? Ask God for clarity and direction.

◇————————————————————————————————◇

◇————————————————————————————————◇

Proverbs 21:5 BSB
"The plans of the diligent bring plenty, as surely as haste leads to poverty."

Avoid haste in your speech. Think before you speak. Avoid haste in your work and plans. Instead, be diligent, steady, and persistent in all you do.

Diligence is one of the 7 virtues we talked about in Proverbs 8, and it indicates your work ethic.

Proverbs 29:20 BSB
"Do you see a man who speaks in haste? There is more hope for a fool than for him."

How can you be diligent this week?
Ideas:
- wake up 30 minutes earlier, go to bed 30 minutes earlier
- put God first by committing your day to Him
- make goals that you desire to achieve
- be intentional, focused, and purposeful
- learn to say no, don't overcommit
- manage your time by planning out your day
- arrive on time to appointments

◇————————————————————————————————◇

◇————————————————————————————————◇

◇————————————————————————————————◇

◇————————————————————————————————◇

p: Diligent Not Hasty

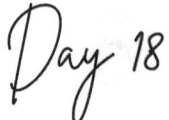

Time Management

Time management is really activity management because that is what you plug into time slots. We all have 168 hours every week. Do a self-audit on how you spend your time.

Don't say that you don't have enough time. Instead, say that you are valuing something else more. We always find time to do what we want to do.

Where do you spend your time?

_____

Who do you spend it with?

_____

Where do you spend your money? This tells you what is important to you.

_____

Don't allow the urgent to crowd out the important - time with God and your family.

_____

What are time wasters?

_____

Successful time managers know that if you don't control your time, others will control it for you.

Take control of the parts of your life that you can control. Write down what you can control:

_____

What do you need to include, and what needs to go?

_____

What do you need to say no to?

_____

Why are you doing_____? Is it getting you closer to your objective/goal?

_____

p: Diligent Not Hasty

Time Management Continued

At the end-of-the day, how is your energy?

How much time did you spend staring at your email or scrolling on social media, and when did you do it (During the time when you are at your best)? Don't use your most effective working hours on time wasters.

One way to control your emails, is to control when you look at them. Another way to control your emails is to silence alerts and notifications while you are working on a project/task.

Be clear and concise in writing your emails:
- Subject line on an email: What is coming up and what you want them to do. For example, "Meeting notes need your input/comments" and "Decision needed on ___"
- IN every communication answer what the reader is asking themselves - What is this and what does it have to do with me?

Time Block. We will cover time blocking on Day 28. Time blocking and writing down tasks and lists helps you organize and prioritize.

Know the 80/20 rule. This will allow you to prioritize your highest-impact tasks.
- 80% of outcomes (or outputs) result from 20% of all causes (or inputs) for any given event
- Out of your entire task list, completing 20% of those tasks will result in 80% of the impact you can create for that day. Identify which tasks have the most impact for your team and focus on those for the day. You will do this on day 28 under Time tracking.

Spiritually
- God has put eternity into man's heart. Ecclesiastes 3:11.
- Number your days to gain a heart of wisdom. Psalm 90:12
- Put God first. Seek first the Kingdom of God and His righteousness, and off of these things shall be added to you. Matthew 6:33
- Don't forget, 15 minutes with the Lord is better than 250 hours elsewhere.

p: Diligent Not Hasty

Notes:

Reputation

Your reputation in life and business is extremely important. A good reputation is better than gold.

"Choose a good reputation over great riches; being held in high esteem is better than silver or gold." Proverbs 22:1 NLT

Be humble before the Lord. True humility and fear of the Lord lead to riches, honor, and long life.

In business, having a good reputation is a valuable asset and will set you apart from your competitors. Also, think of your brand as your reputation.

A business that has a good reputation will attract more customers, leaders, employees, and investors.

Ways to build a good reputation in business:
1. Be honest and transparent
2. Show kindness
3. Give more than what's expected
4. Keep your word
5. Serve
6. Do what is right and just
7. Work hard
8. Plan well
9. Hire well (don't befriend or hire angry, hot-tempered people)
10. Establish a culture of honor: Set the expectation of respect in the organization regardless of title.

Along with a culture of honor in your organization, here are some tips to establish a healthy work environment for your employees:

1. Your employees need to love the company
2. Clearly define objectives for each employee and what the employee needs to do in order to achieve a high grade
3. Have each employee set and commit to 3-5 goals for 6 months and then for 1 year. And then let them go (don't micromanage).
4. Hold quarterly reviews

p: Build A Good Reputation

Stewardship

When *stewardship* first appeared in English during the Middle Ages, it functioned as a job description, denoting the office of a *steward*, or manager of a large household. - Merriam Webster Dictionary

God gives us resources to steward (manage). We carefully and responsibly manage God's money, land, homes, and resources. When we are faithful with little, He gives more.

Genesis 2:15
"Then the Lord God took the man and put him into the garden of Eden to cultivate it and keep it."

The wise have wealth and luxury, but fools spend whatever they get. The wise steward what the Lord gives them. The wise invest money and resources for multiplication. And they love to give to others.

Proverbs 15:27 BSB "He who is greedy for unjust gain brings trouble on his household, but he who hates bribes will live."

Fools will spend whatever they earn without thinking. Fools don't invest or give, they only spend whatever they get. They are selfish and will end in poverty.

Steward your money well with a cheerful heart. Every year my husband and I set a goal of how much money we will give to others. We receive great joy in our hearts when we accomplish the goal. God loves a cheerful giver 2 Corinthians 9:7. Plan out what you will give to others this year, whether it is time, money, or something else.

p: Build A Good Reputation

Notes:

p: Build Your Business

Building your Business

A house is built by wisdom and becomes strong through good sense.
A family is built by wisdom and becomes strong through good sense.
A business is built by wisdom and becomes strong through good sense.

Get Wisdom
Don't start anything without wisdom. Use good sense. Don't envy evil people or desire their company, for they have no future.

Obtain Knowledge
Obtain knowledge for that will fill your rooms, your home, and your business with riches and valuables.

Plan and Prepare Your Fields Before Building
For example, if you were building a home you would hire contractors, architects, and designers. You would need a land survey, budget, and blueprints for construction. You would have an end vision and steps to build that vision.

For your business, you would have a business plan, a sales plan, and a marketing plan to help you reach your vision.

A business plan helps you identify all risks and opportunities of the venture. Planning helps you determine how much money you will need to start the business, your competitive advantage, and more. It is valuable to include your 'why" and values in your business plan.

What are your competitive advantages as a person?

◇————————————————————————————◇

◇————————————————————————————◇

◇————————————————————————————◇

What are your business's competitive advantages?

◇————————————————————————————◇

◇————————————————————————————◇

◇————————————————————————————◇

p: Build Your Business

This is a great time to complete a **SWOT** analysis for yourself and your business. A SWOT analysis will ignite your creativity for new products or directions and help you make decisions:

Strengths:
- What is your competitive advantage?
- What is your business's competitive advantage?
- What's your unique selling or value proposition?

Weaknesses:
Remember, even in your weakness Christ will make you strong, and He will give you insight and guidance. Hire the right people and delegate tasks. Even a weakness can become an opportunity! Questions to ask:

- What business processes need improvement?
- Do your supplies come from one supplier/location?
- What technology needs to be updated?
- Does one customer make up more than 10% of your business?
- What expertise do you lack?
- What tasks do you need to delegate?

Opportunities:
- Are there additional products your customers want that you could provide?

p: Build Your Business

Threats:
Minimize threats and risk with risk management.

Risk Management tips in business:
- Hire an experienced business coach or mentor to prevent beginner mistakes
- Have an insurance policy in place
- Use the bootstrapping method to prove your model
- Have savings to cover 3 months of expenses (Economic Risk)
- Build and maintain your reputation and monitor what people are saying about your business both online and offline

Are there any upcoming law or regulation changes that will impact us?
- Research the applicable laws for your business so you are compliant

How easy is it for someone to poach key employees?
- Create a culture of honor, set expectations, have systems in place for all employees to use, have employees set and commit to goals, and be transparent
- Develop a non-compete agreement

p: Build Your Business

Notes:

Have Wise Mentors and Friends

"The heartfelt counsel of a friend is as sweet as perfume and incense." Proverbs 27:9 NLT

"As iron sharpens iron, so a friend sharpens a friend." Proverbs 27:17 NLT

The Importance of Friends and Mentors:

1. Keep us Accountable

If we have trusted friends and advisors, they will provide warnings and we will receive their warnings because we know they have our best interests in mind. They will hold us accountable for our character and actions.

2. Motivate and Encourage

Friends and mentors offer motivation and encouragement. If you fall down, they are there to pick you up.

Ecclesiastes 4:9-10 ESV "Two are better than one, because they have a good reward for their toil. For if they fall, one will lift up his fellow. But woe to him who is alone when he falls and has not another to lift him up!

3. Make us More Effective

As the above verse states, two are better than one because they get more done by working together. They have a good reward for their toil. Mentors have experience and expertise to help with making wise decisions and help with business deals.

Do you have wise mentors and friends?

◇————————————————————————————◇

Are you a wise friend and mentor to someone?

◇————————————————————————————◇

If you need a wise mentor, ask the Lord to highlight a person for you:

◇————————————————————————————◇

p: Target Market

Day 22

Your Target Market

Your Target Market is also known as your who, niche, or micro-niche.

Identify who your business will serve. This is your target market. These are your people. Your business/service isn't for everyone. Be clear and concise on your target market.

How To Find Your Who/Target Market
What do you enjoy doing?

What are your skills and talents?

Look back at times in your life when you helped other people and felt fulfilled.

What type of people catch your attention? For example, you might notice athletes or artists. You might notice people who have a physical ailment. Write down the kind of people who catch your attention:

What kind of people are you helping right now, or have helped in the past?

Study your WHO. Write out the attributes and pain points of your target market.

A pain point is a specific problem that prospective customers of your business are experiencing.

52

p: Target Market

Your Target Market

What does your target market do in their free time? What are their interests?

_____

_____

What are the demographics of your target market?

_____

_____

Here are tips on researching your target market:

- Look at Google Analytics and social media insights to identify your target market in terms of demographics. Enable the demographic and interest reports in Google Analytics.
- Review message boards, forums and facebook groups to discover what your target market is asking.

_____

_____

_____

_____

_____

_____

_____

_____

p: Target Market

Your Target Market Continued:

What problem are you solving? What outcome are you promising?

<hr>

<hr>

Resolve pain and/or create delight!

What are some of the current desires, dreams, fears, or problems of your WHO?

<hr>

<hr>

<hr>

How does your process, product, or service solve that problem?

<hr>

<hr>

<hr>

How can you love and serve your WHO even more? Let's go above and beyond for our WHO and what they are asking for! Going above and beyond what your WHO asks for will set you apart from your competitors.

<hr>

<hr>

<hr>

Validate your idea.
Do a test run to make sure there is a paying market for your service or product.

<hr>

<hr>

<hr>

<hr>

p: Target Market

Notes:

Marketing Tips

What is Marketing?
Marketing is the process of finding out the needs, wants, and pain points of your customer and then creating and delivering value to meet their need and solve their problem.

It is a process:
Research
Promote
Sell
Distribute

If you own your own business or want to start your own business, here are some marketing tips:

Identify your target market
- create a customer profile
- what is your target customer's age, interests, gender, etc?
- look at your target market (who) page in this workbook

Identify your competitors
- what sets you apart from your competitors (competitive advantage)
- differentiate yourself

What specialized knowledge and experience do you have?

_____

_____

Determine your price point
- look at price information from the current market
- service trumps price, so if you have exceptional service your price point can be the same or higher than your competitors

Use social media channels
- determine which channels are best for your industry

Keep and use what is already working for you
- To save time, money, energy, and resources, keep strategies that are successful

p: Marketing

Marketing Tips Continued

Network
- love people
- help and give to others
- attend conferences in your industry

Luke 6:38
"Give, and it will be given to you. A good measure, pressed down, shaken together and running over, will be poured into your lap. For with the measure you use, it will be measured to you."

Build an email list
- email campaigns to communicate events and promotions
- text campaigns

Use leverage
- system leverages include customer relationship management software (CRM)
- financial leverage (investors)
- counter your weaknesses by hiring someone who is strong in that area

Positive Messaging
- speak in positives
- speak about future
- hopeful language

Write down one or two marketing tips you can implement today, this month and this year:

◇———————————————————————————◇

◇———————————————————————————◇

◇———————————————————————————◇

◇———————————————————————————◇

p: Marketing

Notes:

p: Set and Achieve Goals

Goal Setting

When people do not seek and accept divine guidance, they run wild. But whoever obeys the law is joyful. God has divine guidance for you. Ask the Lord for divine goals and guidance. Know that goal setting is more than making a list of goals and checking the boxes as you complete them. God's divine guidance will help you develop a way to live well, serve, and succeed. Goal setting helps you develop a prosperous lifestyle.

Prosper means to become strong and to flourish and succeed in an activity. 3 John 1:2 AMP "Beloved, I pray that in every way you may succeed and prosper and be in good health [physically], just as [I know] your soul prospers [spiritually]."

God wants us to succeed and prosper in every way! He wants us to be in good health physically and spiritually. Make goals for your business, family, faith, and health. Decide what you want in each of those areas.

"In life, the first thing you must do is decide what you really want. Weigh the costs and the results. Are the results worthy of the costs? Then make up your mind completely and go after your goal with all your might." — Alfred A. Montapert

- What do you want in life, business, health, and faith?

  ◇───◇

  ◇───◇

- Will the benefit outweigh the cost?

  ◇───◇

- Keep and use what is already working for you. This will save you time. Every new thing you take on has a learning curve and an opportunity cost. Opportunity costs include energy, time, and money.

  ◇───◇

  ◇───◇

p: Set and Achieve Goals

Goal Setting Continued

- Start with what was previously successful.

  ◇————————————————————————◇

  ◇————————————————————————◇

- Separate long-term, short-term, and daily goals. And always keep the vision upfront. Use your vision board.

  ◇————————————————————————◇

  ◇————————————————————————◇

- Long-term goals. Example: in 10 years, business cash flows $10,000/mo or in 5 years, business cash flows $5,000/mo.
  Write out one long-term goal:

  ◇————————————————————————◇

  ◇————————————————————————◇

- Short-term goals. Example: in 1 year, business cash flows $1,000/mo.
  Write out one short-term goal:

  ◇————————————————————————◇

  ◇————————————————————————◇

- Monthly goals. Example: post 20 videos on youtube for my business, and develop my business plan.
  Write out one monthly goal:

  ◇————————————————————————◇

  ◇————————————————————————◇

- Daily goals. Example: meet with my mentor, and listen to a podcast.
  Write out a daily goal:

  ◇————————————————————————◇

  ◇————————————————————————◇

p: Set and Achieve Goals

Notes:

p: Protect Your Heart

Guard Your Heart

"A stone is heavy and sand is weighty, but the resentment caused by a fool is even heavier. Anger is cruel, and wrath is like a flood, but jealousy is even more dangerous."
Proverbs 27:3-4 NLT

Jealousy is dangerous. There is no need to be jealous of others as there is only one of you. No one else can do what you do or how you do it. God gave you a unique personality, ability, and talent.

Write out who you are in Christ, including your unique personality, abilities, and talents:

_____

_____

_____

PERSONALITY	ABILITIES	TALENTS

p: Protect Your Heart

As a face is reflected in water, so the heart reflects the real person.

From your heart flows everything in life. Proverbs 4:23 NIV says, "Above all else, guard your heart, for everything you do flows from it."

Here are four ways to guard your heart:
1. Continually fill your heart with truth. God's word is truth (John 17:17) and Jesus is the Truth (John 14:6). Read and meditate on God's word day and night.
2. Think on what is good, true, honorable, just, pure, lovely, gracious and excellent (Philippians 4:8)
3. Say out loud positive declarations and declare God's promises over yourself. Faith comes by hearing
4. Pray and be thankful. Philippians 4:6-7 tells us to not be anxious about anything, but in everything by prayer and supplication with thanksgiving let our requests be made known to God. And the peace of God, which passes all understanding, will guard your heart and mind in Christ Jesus.

How is the condition of your heart?

◇——————————————————————————————◇

◇——————————————————————————————◇

What you speak comes from your heart. If you are holding on to resentment and bitterness, then that will flow from your heart and defile you. Release forgiveness to anyone who has hurt you and ask God to remove any bitterness or resentment. When you forgive someone, you release a prisoner. And that prisoner is you.

◇——————————————————————————————◇

◇——————————————————————————————◇

◇——————————————————————————————◇

◇——————————————————————————————◇

◇——————————————————————————————◇

◇——————————————————————————————◇

p: Protect Your Heart

Also, dreams come from your heart, so you want and need a new, whole heart. A whole heart brings whole dreams. A whole heart is a healthy heart that does not have any unforgiveness, hurt, anger, bitterness or resentment in it.

Ask God to take any hurt from your heart that could be blocking your dreams.

_____

_____

_____

_____

Do you know that God gives you a new heart when you are born again (Ezekiel 36:26)? He puts His Spirit in you and gives you a heart of flesh. This means He takes your hard heart and gives you a new heart that is soft and responsive to His Spirit's guidance.

"The good man brings good things out of the good treasure of his heart, and the evil man brings evil things out of the evil treasure of his heart. For out of the overflow of the heart, the mouth speaks." Luke 6:45 BSB

Guarding your heart includes guarding your feelings, will, and intellect. As you guard your feelings, your will, and your intellect, life will flow from you. Strength will flow from you.

Ask the Lord to keep your heart tender and responsive to his nudges. Follow the nudges because they lead to life, success, and good fruit!

_____

_____

_____

_____

_____

_____

_____

_____

p: Protect Your Heart

Notes:

Be The Standard of Excellence In Your Industry

In life and in business, don't turn your back on what you know is right. When we turn our back on what we know is right, we dull our conscience. Soon we won't be able to discern what is right from wrong.

Do what is right and be obedient. The trustworthy person will get a rich reward, but a person who wants quick riches will get into trouble.

Set the standard of excellence in your industry. The Holy Spirit is your best success coach and will give you divine strategy and next-level energy. Don't hold back on who God created you to be. You will save and transform lives through your success.

Go above and beyond your offer to your customer.

God pours His Spirit out on all flesh. There are no limits with the Lord. Anything is possible with Him! The Lord will give you visions and dreams to achieve your purpose, just as He did for Joseph. Don't let your vision become stuck. Your current reality is your starting point. Know where you are starting from and where you are going.

 Joseph had a big dream that was beyond his current circumstance. His purpose and dream offended his brothers. Your purpose will offend some people, but people can't control you, and your purpose isn't for them. Don't give up. Never give up.

Joseph had a second dream that was even more powerful than the first! May the Lord give you multiple dreams for your purpose.

What are some of the dreams that you are holding in your heart?

<hr/>
<hr/>

What deserves more of your attention? Is It your current reality or your dreams? Both your current reality and dreams will be hard work. Do you want to stay in your current reality, or focus on your dreams?

<hr/>
<hr/>

p: Standard of Excellence

Notes:

p: You Are Royalty

Royal Posture

The godly are as bold as a lion. A lion postures itself and walks with a stately stride. A lion is confident and won't run away from anything.

Proverbs 30:29-31 NLT says, "There are three things that walk with stately stride— no, four that strut about: the lion, king of animals, who won't turn aside for anything, the strutting rooster, the male goat, a king as he leads his army."

How do you walk? Do you walk with confidence? Do you walk with a stately stride?

You are royalty. You are a King or Queen. You rule and reign with integrity, love, and power. You are strong.

Walk like a leader. Posture yourself as a leader. Stand tall.

We carry and release what we are conscious of, so pay attention to what you are focusing on. Imagine yourself surrounded by God the Father, Son, and Holy Spirit. Not only are you surrounded by the trinity, but the trinity is IN you.

Cut off things that aren't profitable. Cut out negative talk. Cut out strategies that aren't working. Is there anything in your life or business that you need to cut?

◇————————————————————————◇

◇————————————————————————◇

◇————————————————————————◇

Time tracking can help you determine things that aren't working or that could be delegated. Time tracking is another time-management tool to help you manage your time well.

Time track in 30 min intervals for a couple of days and note:
- What activities are low value?

- What activities are high value?

Time Tracking Continued

- What activities can you potentially delegate?

- What systems could replace certain activities?

For example, you may spend a lot of time sharing documents and sending updates to employees. Basecamp is a project management and team communication software that would help you track projects and task progress, communicate with your team, share documents, and facilitate collaboration with them.

- What activities are ones only I have the expertise to complete?

- Identify activities where other people might bring more skill

- What activities aren't profitable?

p: Time Tracking

Time Block	Activity	Notes

p: Time Tracking

Time Block	Activity	Notes

p: Destiny

Discover Your Destiny

God created you for something special. "For we are God's masterpiece. He has created us anew in Christ Jesus, so we can do the good things he planned for us long ago." Ephesians 2:10 NLT

You are unique. You are an original, one-of-a-kind masterpiece.

God prepared in advance the good works for you to complete. He has good plans for you and puts desires in your heart to fulfill. He is speaking to you and giving you new discoveries. These new discoveries are the solutions to the world's greatest problems. Dream with the Lord. He is giving you His higher level thinking and His higher ways.

Work diligently and urgently:
- God is giving you a divine blueprint just for you
- Count your days, or as Ecclesiastes says, seize the day
- Your power of success is connected to your passion and your why. Find your source of passion and know your why behind what you are doing
- Pay attention to the patterns in your life and your inward feelings. For example, when I talk about business, real estate and restoration of homes and people, I am excited. I come alive and feel an energy surge.

What drives you?

What are the patterns in your life?

What problems are you seeing today that keep you up at night?

What types of people draw your attention?

What makes you excited?

p: Destiny

Notes:

Have Vision

What do you see in the future? What are the dreams and imaginations in your heart? Write down what you see in the future for your life and your business. What are your dreams? What you see is what you get! Dream BIG.

It's time to dream and create. God gives you power to create your tomorrow. Here is a top trait of elite entrepreneurs: They take 100% responsibility for their life. They know they can create, design, and build whatever life they want. They make moves, not excuses. They never stop learning and growing.

Do you believe anything is possible? Do you believe you can create your tomorrow? Don't doubt. Doubt is undecided belief, which means you will go back and forth without moving forward. Mark 9:23 says, "Everything is possible for those who believe." What is everything for you? Write down your vision and the definition of everything:

_____

_____

_____

What do you want? Take time and let that desire rise up in you! Desire will lead to creativity.

_____

_____

_____

_____

What are you dissatisfied with? Combine your desire and dissatisfaction and write it down.

_____

_____

_____

I declare new ways and favor over you! Your dreams are possible!

p: Destiny

Notes:

What does mastering your domain look like?

In Proverbs 31, we meet a woman who sums up all of Proverbs. She operates in wisdom and rules and reigns in life and business. She leads with integrity and noble character.

Owns a Business
She goes to inspect a field and buys it with her earnings. Then, she plants a vineyard. This is her business.

Researches and Plans
She is wise and inspects the field before she buys it. She does her due diligence. She is savvy in the marketplace.

Stewards Her Resources
She saved and worked so that with her earnings she could plant a vineyard to produce food and product.

Has Personality
She is energetic and strong.

Hard Worker
She makes sure her dealings are profitable; her lamp burns late into the night. She isn't lazy.

Generous
She extends a helping hand to the poor.

Healthy and Successful Family
Her husband is well known at the city gates, where he sits with the other civic leaders. She is clothed with strength and dignity, and she laughs without fear of the future.

Wise
When she speaks, her words are wise, and she gives instructions with kindness. She carefully watches everything in the household. She makes belted linen garments and sashes to sell to the merchants. This is another stream of revenue she created with her hands.

p: Master Your Domain

What skills and talents do you possess?

_____

_____

_____

Who is currently in your network?

_____

_____

_____

What resources do you possess? Are there things you want to add?

_____

_____

_____

The Proverbs 31 woman doesn't fear the future. She fears God. She does not have "poverty thinking" in her life. She masters her domain. She is ruling and reigning and in control of her domain.

Think life-giving thoughts. Think positively. Think of possibilities. Jesus is life. He wants to give you solutions to bring change.

Ask Him what He sees. Then take a moment to focus and reflect on the life-giving thoughts, ideas, and possibilities He shows you.

_____

_____

_____

_____

_____

_____

Notes:

p: Master Your Domain

God wants to bless you extravagantly. He wants you to be famous, yes legendary. Think bigger and advance. You are going from strength to strength and glory to glory. He is setting you high above all the nations of the earth.

"And if you faithfully obey the voice of the Lord your God, being careful to do all his commandments that I command you today, the Lord your God will set you high above all the nations of the earth. And all these blessings shall come upon you and overtake you, if you obey the voice of the Lord your God. Blessed shall you be in the city, and blessed shall you be in the field. Blessed shall be the fruit of your womb and the fruit of your ground and the fruit of your cattle, the increase of your herds and the young of your flock. Blessed shall be your basket and your kneading bowl. Blessed shall you be when you come in, and blessed shall you be when you go out." Deuteronomy 28:1-6

God wants you to be confident, strong and courageous. God will not fail you.

"This Book of the Law shaw not depart from your mouth, but you shall read [and meditate on] it day and night, so that you may be careful to do [everything] in accordance with all that is written in it; for then you will make your way prosperous, and then you will be successful." Joshua 1:8 AMP

Take your place of royalty. Listen to the Lord. He will make your way prosperous, and you will be successful.

God bless you and keep you. The Lord is with you.

It's Go Time!